W9-BOO-903

OUR WILD™
WORLD
SERIES

Polar Bears

NorthWord Press
Chanhassen, Minnesota

To Kathy Feeney for all her generous help, and to Nancy Rosanoff, intuition teacher extraordinaire.
Special thanks to Scott Schliebe of the U.S. Fish and Wildlife Service in Alaska,
Steve Amstrup, Barbara Nielsen, and Cindy Bickel.

—L. T.

Illustrations by John F. McGee
Designed by Russell S. Kuepper
Edited by Aimee Jackson

NorthWord Press
18705 Lake Drive East
Chanhassen, MN 55317
1-800-328-3895
www.northwordpress.com

Library of Congress Cataloging-in-Publication Data

Tagliaferro, Linda.
    Polar Bears / Linda Tagliaferro ; illustrations by John F. McGee.
        p. cm. -- (Our wild world series)
    ISBN 1-55971-829-3 (hardcover) -- ISBN 1-55971-828-5 (softcover)
        1. Polar bear--Juvenile literature. I. McGee, John F. II. Title. III. Series.

QL737.C27 T328 2002
599.786--dc21   2002019008

Printed in Singapore

10 9 8 7 6 5 4 3 2 1

Our **WILD**™
W🌐RLD
SERIES

Polar Bears

Linda Tagliaferro
Illustrations by John F. McGee

NORTHWORD PRESS
Chanhassen, Minnesota

POLAR BEARS are cool animals. But it's not just because they are fun to learn about. Polar bears live in the coastal areas of the Arctic—the areas around the North Pole—at the top of the world. These are lands of snow, ice, and freezing cold water. There are heavy snowstorms, freezing temperatures, and cold, harsh winds in these lands. Very few animals could survive in places like this, but to the polar bear, this area is a comfortable home.

The mighty polar bear is the largest meat eater that lives on land.

Two polar bear cubs, or babies, follow their mother closely. Female polar bears give birth about every three years.

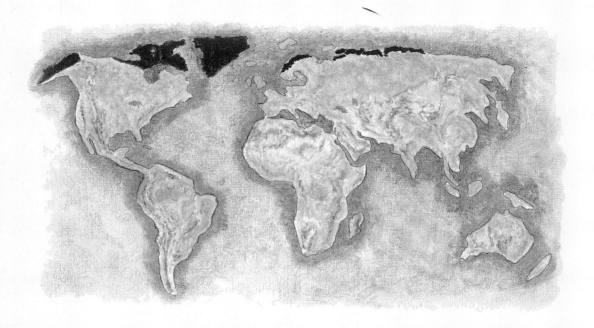

There are areas in five countries in the far north where polar bears roam: Alaska in the United States, the northern part of Canada, Greenland (an island owned by Denmark), some islands in Norway, and Russia.

These amazing bears are the largest members of the bear family. Only Alaskan brown bears can sometimes grow as big as polar bears. There are eight species (SPEE-sees), or kinds, of bears, and some scientists think that the polar bear is the most recent to develop. Some scientists think that the polar bears are the distant relatives of the brown bears that lived in an area near Siberia (sy-BEER-ee-uh) in eastern Russia.

Polar bears are also the largest carnivores (KAR-nuh-vorz), or meat eaters, on land. The males can stand up to 10 feet (3 meters) tall on their hind legs. That's taller than a school bus! Males can weigh over 1,000 pounds (454 kilograms). Adult females are much smaller than the males and can be about 6 to 8 feet (1.8 to 2.4 meters) tall. That's still bigger than a tall basketball player! Female polar bears weigh about 500 pounds (227 kilograms).

These mighty animals have shorter arms and legs than other bears, but they have tremendously strong muscles. Their heads and ears are smaller than most bears', and they only have a very small tail. Larger ears and tails would stick out and get cold quickly in the freezing Arctic climate. The polar bear's ears are rounded and have fur on the inside to protect against the cold. It's like having built-in earmuffs!

Polar bears stand on their hind legs to get a better view or to pick up the scent of food. They can even walk on two legs for short distances.

Polar bears like to curl up when they sleep to keep warm. They sleep about 7 or 8 hours at a time, just like humans, and they also take short naps during the day to conserve energy.

In the winter when hunting is good, a polar bear might gain over 200 pounds (90 kilograms). In the summer when food is scarce, it will get its energy from all the fat that it has stored.

Temperatures in the Arctic can go down as low as -50 degrees Fahrenheit (-45 degrees Celsius) in the winter. Luckily for the polar bear, its body is well built for survival in cold weather. In order to keep warm, the polar bear has a "coat" of thick white fur. There are actually two layers of fur. The lower layer is like thick, oily wool, and the top hairs are long and hollow. They keep the bear warm by holding in some air like a fluffy down comforter.

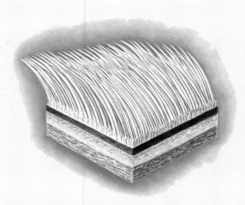

The bear's white fur helps it to blend into the snow and ice. But its fur is actually colorless. The bear's fur looks white because it reflects the light from the sun. Sometimes, the bear's fur looks yellowish-white because the sunlight has changed its color. The polar bear's skin is all black, but it can't be seen because of all its fur. The dark color helps to hold in the heat from sunlight. The eyes, nose, and tongue of the polar bear are also black.

Another reason that polar bears keep warm in the cold is because they have a layer of blubber, or fat, inside their bodies. The layer of blubber can be as thick as 4½ inches (11.5 centimeters). To keep this layer of fat, a polar bear must eat fatty foods, like one seal a week. A polar bear can eat about 100 pounds (45.3 kilograms) of blubber at just one meal. That's like a 90-pound (40.8 kilogram) human child eating 9 pounds (4 kilograms) of animal fat for dinner!

Polar Bear
FUNFACT:

The scientific name for the polar bear, *Ursus maritimus*, means "sea bear" in Latin.

A polar bear's inside layer of blubber helps to keep it warm when it swims in icy waters.

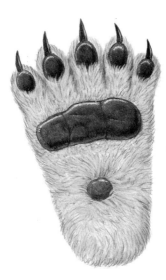

The bear's paws are very large and look like big furry slippers. The front paws are round and a little larger than its long back paws. The front paws are about 12 inches (30.5 centimeters) wide. That's bigger than a school notebook! These big paws are used as powerful weapons for attacking the bear's prey (PRAY)—the animals that it kills for food. There are black pads that are as rough as sandpaper on the bottom of all of its paws. These coarse pads, together with the thick white fur on the bottom of the bear's feet, help to keep it from slipping on the ice and snow. There are also small bumps on the bottom of the bear's paws to help it get a good grip on the ice.

The polar bear's front paws are webbed like ducks' feet. These paws act like flippers and help the bear to swim. These Arctic bears are just as comfortable on land as they are in the water. They are excellent swimmers and can even stay underwater for a minute or two. They sometimes need to swim to get where they want to go. In the summer when the ice begins to melt, polar bears may get stuck out on a floating piece of ice. Then they have to jump in the water and swim to shore. They can swim at a speed of 6 miles per hour (9.6 kilometers per hour), and can dive as deep as 15 feet (4.5 meters) below the water's surface. Their long necks help them to keep their heads out of the icy water as they paddle along.

On land a polar bear usually walks slowly—about 3 miles per hour (4.8 kilometers per hour). It can run up to 25 miles per hour (40 kilometers per hour), but it gets tired quickly. Because it has thick fur on the outside and a layer of blubber on the inside, the polar bear overheats, or gets too hot, if it runs fast.

To survive in the Arctic, polar bears must be good hunters. They have longer snouts than most bears, and they have a superb sense of smell. They sometimes hold their noses high in the air or stand on their hind legs to sniff the air for prey, which can be miles away. Their eyesight is sharp, and their hearing is also excellent.

They have longer, sharper teeth than other bears. This is important because they are meat eaters. Their claws are sharp and curved and hold tightly onto their prey. There are five claws on each of the polar bear's paws, and they can be 2 inches (5 centimeters) long. The claws also make it easier to walk on the slippery ice.

A mother polar bear and her two cubs sniff the air.
They can smell a seal more than 1 mile (1.6 kilometers) away.

A polar bear tramples the snow and digs deep
to hunt for a ringed seal pup.

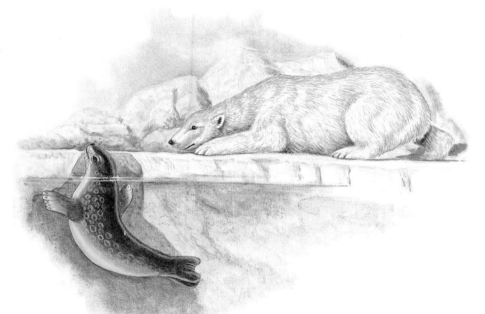

Polar bears eat more meat than any other bears. They have extra-large stomachs to help them digest their meals. The polar bear's favorite food is a type of seal called the ringed seal. It is the smallest seal in the Arctic and measures about 4 feet (1.2 meters) in length. An average ringed seal weighs about 150 pounds (68 kilograms). They are plump because they have a thick layer of blubber under their skin. Ringed seals swim in the cold Arctic waters, but they have to come up for air. The seals use the sharp nails on their flippers to scratch out holes in the ice. They swim up to these openings, called breathing holes, and poke their heads up for air every 5 to 15 minutes. This is when polar bears try to catch them with one quick swipe of their powerful paws.

If the polar bears are very quiet, the seals may not hear them, or see them, because the bears are camouflaged (KAM-uh-flajd) against the white snow. Since their fur is the same color, it blends into the background and makes the bears hard to see. The seals have many different breathing holes, so they might not use one right away. The polar bears must be patient. They may have to wait for hours before a ringed seal appears. But even when a seal appears, it might hear or catch sight of the bear at the last minute and escape by swimming under the ice. A polar bear might only be successful in 1 out of 20 hunts.

After catching a seal, a polar bear eats only the skin and fat and leaves the rest of the meat. Scavengers (SKAV-in-jers), any animals that look for leftover food, usually eat the remains of the bear's meal. Arctic foxes, for example, sometimes follow a polar bear after its hunt. They wait until the bear is finished with its meal and then feast on the seal meat that is left over. Young bears that are not as successful at hunting may also join in. Arctic birds like ravens and Ivory gulls then finish off any meat that is left on the seal's bones.

Polar bears also eat the rich blubber of walruses, but they must fight hard for this food. Some adult male walruses may weigh up to 3,000 pounds (1,360 kilograms), and they can injure or kill a polar bear by attacking it with their enormous, dangerous tusks. Usually the bears only succeed at catching young, small walruses. Sometimes they might find a dead adult walrus on the ice.

Arctic foxes closely follow a polar bear,
hoping to get the remains of a successful hunt.

Polar bears prefer to hunt by sitting and waiting because they overheat quickly when they run.

In order to hunt for seals, polar bears need to wait on the ice. In the Arctic summer, some of the ice melts and this makes it hard for the bears to catch their food. The seals are usually farther out in the water. So at this time, polar bears eat what they can. They look for birds like snow geese or eat their eggs. They use their sharp sense of smell to locate the carcasses (KAR-kus-iz), or dead bodies, of whales, fish, or other animals that have washed up on the ice. If they are very hungry in the summer, they may eat berries and plants that they find on land. They may even eat tiny lemmings, small Arctic animals that look like mice with short tails. Sometimes they do not eat for several months.

A mother bear watches out for her cubs while they eat food that she hunted for the three of them. The mother bear must eat enough to produce milk for her growing cubs.

Scientists can tell what kind of food a polar bear has just eaten by looking at its droppings, or scat. Sometimes there will be fur from a ringed seal in the bear's scat.

A polar bear may seem like a sloppy eater, getting blood and fat all over its fur as it feeds. But when it's finished eating, it spends time cleaning itself. It might wash itself by jumping in the water, or it might lick itself clean in much the same way that a cat does. This neatness isn't just to make the polar bear's fur look good. If the polar bear's fur gets wet or matted down with dirt, it can't protect against the cold. The fur needs to stand up straight so it can trap the air and hold the heat in. The fur needs to stay as clean as possible at all times.

This polar bear shakes itself off after a swim.
Polar bears also drag themselves across the ice to dry off.

These adult polar bears gather in Churchill, Manitoba, in Canada. The town is known as "The Polar Bear Capital of the World" because every October and November many polar bears go there to wait for the ice to freeze over.

The polar bear is a wanderer. In the summer when the ice begins to melt, some bears travel north where the weather is colder and there is more ice. Then they go south in the winter as the ice begins to freeze again. During the coldest months, the polar bear must eat a great deal and put on a lot of weight. If not, it could starve to death during the warm months when food is scarce. The extra weight acts like fuel for the bear's body when it can't find enough food to eat.

During their migration (my-GRAY-shun), or moving from one area to another, polar bears may travel hundreds or even thousands of miles. But they usually go back to the places where they learned to hunt when they were cubs, or baby bears. This is called their territory, or home range. A polar bear's home range is much larger than the ranges of any other kind of bear. They might be anywhere from 20,000 square miles (51,000 square kilometers) to 135,000 square miles (350,650 square kilometers). Even though home ranges might overlap, polar bears do not fight over their territories.

Polar bears usually travel alone, but in some places, like Churchill in Manitoba, Canada, large groups of polar bears gather around Hudson Bay in the late fall. They are waiting for the weather to get colder. Then when the water freezes, the polar bears roam the ice looking for seals that come up at breathing holes.

Polar Bear
FUNFACT:

The powerful jaws of polar bears have 42 teeth to grip their prey. Adult humans have 32 teeth.

Polar bears look ferocious, but they can be quite playful with each other. They can grab hold of each other and wrestle, but they are not trying to hurt one another. They are just having fun! This also helps to prepare them for real fighting. If another polar bear attacks them, they will know the right moves to defend themselves. They also learn from play-fighting which other bears are too strong for them. They will keep away from them in a real fight.

When a polar bear wants to play, it shakes its head from side to side to let another bear know it is in the mood for a fighting game. Both young bears and adult bears play. They might stand up on their hind legs, with their front paws down and their chins next to their chests, to get ready to tackle another playful bear.

Even though polar bears can be playful, there are times when they are very serious. There is no mistaking a bear that is not in the mood for play. Growling, roaring, and hissing warn other bears that they should stay away. When a polar bear lowers its head and lays its ears back, it is also a sign that it's not in a good mood.

These two adult male polar bears are play-fighting.
This does not hurt the bears, and it teaches them real fighting skills
they will need later to compete for females.

Bears also have ways of showing each other good manners, too. If a large bear is eating, a younger or smaller one might want the leftovers. A well-mannered young bear gets low to the ground and silently comes close to the larger bear who is eating. Then, the smaller bear quietly circles around the food. It shyly begs for food by gently touching noses with the dining bear and often gets what it wants if it acts politely in this way.

In the spring, usually in April or May, female polar bears give off a scent in their urine that tells the male bears that they are ready to mate. With their sharp sense of smell, many of the males follow the females. The eager males fight to see who is the strongest, and only this one earns the right to mate with the female. The winning male and the female stay together for about a week, but then the female's scent changes. She ignores the male, and he goes off, looking for another female that is ready to mate.

Polar bears have long necks, and their front legs are much longer than their back legs.

An angry polar bear growls to warn other bears to stay far away.

This hole in the snow shows where a mother bear and her cubs came out of their den. There is a short tunnel and usually one main room, but sometimes there can be two, or even four smaller rooms in the den.

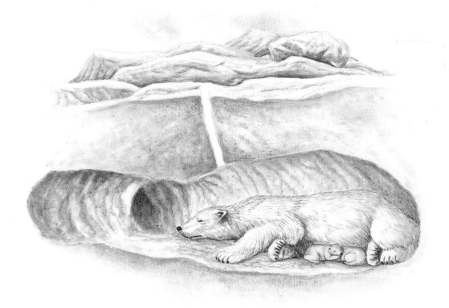

The female bear prepares to give birth to her cubs, or baby bears. She must eat a great deal of food in the next few months. She needs to build up enough fat to last for a long time. She will not be eating for many months, and she might lose half of her weight in that time. In the late fall, she looks for a safe place to dig a den. She usually finds a place that provides some shelter against the raging Arctic winds. To keep out the cold, she digs a long tunnel that leads to a den, which is a resting area. This is the place where she goes into a kind of sleep while her babies develop inside her. She does not eat or drink, or pass water or waste during this time. The den is only about 4 feet (1.2 meters) across and 3 feet (less than a meter) high at the center.

While other types of bears go into hibernation (hi-ber-NAY-shun), which is a long, deep winter sleep, male polar bears do not. They continue to roam around their home range all winter. Although mother polar bears go into a kind of sleep in their den, it is not as deep a sleep as in hibernation. They can wake up more quickly than truly hibernating bears if they sense danger.

A bear cub rests inside its den. Polar bear mothers often dig dens in snowdrifts on mountains to keep warm and far from male bears that can sometimes be dangerous to cubs.

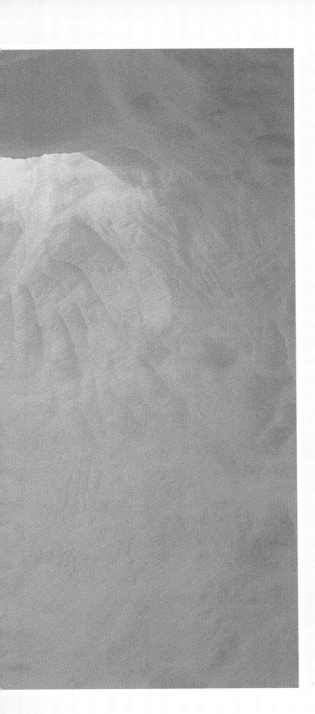

In the winter as the mother bear sleeps, her cubs are born 8 months after she mated. Usually, two cubs are born at the same time, and on rare occasions, three may be born.

At birth, the cubs are only about as big as a kitten, and they weigh about 1 pound (about 0.5 kilogram). They have pink bodies with just a thin coat of short, white hair. Their eyes are closed, and they can't see or hear. They are born without teeth. The cubs depend on their mother for food and warmth. But even though their mother is sleeping, she is still providing for them. Her rich, fatty milk helps them to grow quickly. In just the first month after their birth, the cubs can grow to more than four times their birth weight. At this time, they can open their eyes and see. They can also hear, but they still aren't able to walk around.

By the time that it is two months old, a polar bear cub may be as big as a human baby. Now it has teeth, and it has grown thick white fur. It can walk around in the den by itself, but it is still not strong enough to go out into the harsh surroundings in the outside world. The den is much warmer than the outside air. In the spring when they are about 3 months old, the cubs are ready to come out of the den with their mother. They stay around the den for about 12 days or more, and they sleep there at night.

Staying near the den for this time helps the cubs get used to the cold weather outside and gives them practice walking around in the ice and snow.

The female polar bear is a very good mother. She protects her cubs fiercely if there is danger. Even though females are smaller than male polar bears, a mother bear will lower her head and charge at a male bear that threatens her cubs. She has good reason to do this. Male bears sometimes kill the helpless cubs.

Polar Bear
FUNFACT:

During very severe snowstorms, a polar bear might dig a small hole in the snow. It curls up in this cozy space until the storm passes.

This mother polar bear defends her cubs from an approaching male.
Even though female polar bears are smaller than males, their fierce
behavior usually scares males away from their young.

This mother polar bear is feeding milk to her two cubs. Even though they have thick fur, the cubs do not have an inside layer of fat yet. They need their mother's milk for energy and to keep warm.

There are many dangers in the cold north, such as starvation, disease, and attacks by other animals. Many cubs do not live past their first year. For two or three years, the cubs drink their mother's milk, and they begin to eat meat that their mother has hunted. She must hunt well in order to be able to produce enough food for herself and her cubs.

The cubs stay by their mother's side and learn how to survive in the harsh conditions of the Arctic. Together, the mother bear and her cubs travel down to the sea ice to look for seals to eat. They stop several times a day to rest or for the mother bear to nurse her cubs. The mother digs small shelters in the snow where the cubs can sleep safely.

If the mother bear senses danger and wants her cubs to come to her immediately, she gives out a soft growl to get their attention. They learn how to hunt for ringed seals by watching her as she skillfully catches the plump animals. Sometimes the cubs even help her hunt. The cubs might sit at nearby seal breathing holes. They may not be swift enough or strong enough to catch a seal that needs to come up for air. But if the seal sees them, it may come up for air in another breathing hole, possibly one where the mother bear is waiting.

The mother bear hunts for seal pups as well as adult ringed seals. The pups are born in April or May, and they are called whitecoats. They live in places called birth lairs. This is a covered den under the snow. Polar bears can smell them even if they can't see them under the snow. When the mother bear finds one of these birth lairs, she smashes its roof with her powerful paws and sticks her head into the enclosure to catch the seals inside.

When the cubs have reached the age of 2 or 3, the mother chases them away or abandons them. Now they are all alone and must take care of themselves. If they have learned all the survival skills from their mother, they will be able to hunt successfully on their own. They may travel over 600 miles (965 kilometers) to establish a new home range that is far from their mother's. If they can make it on their own until they are 5 or 6 years old, they will be ready to mate and have families of their own. At the age of 10 or 11, they will reach their adult weight. In the wild, polar bears usually live from 15 to 20 years.

Polar Bear
FUNFACT:

Polar bears do the "dog paddle" when they swim. Their front paws and arms propel them through the water while their back legs and feet lay flat and help them to steer into the direction they want to go.

Polar bear cubs learn to hunt and swim by imitating their mother.

A one-year-old cub follows in its mother's footsteps. Although adult bears can run as fast as a horse, they normally walk slowly to avoid overheating or to allow their cubs to keep up with them.

Scientists who study polar bears in the wild estimate that there are between 22,000 and 25,000 currently living in the Arctic. But there are some serious threats to the bears' existence. Some animals are considered endangered species. This means that they are in danger of dying out forever. Fortunately, the polar bear is not an endangered species. But it is considered a threatened species. This means that there are some problems that might lead to its becoming endangered.

Polar Bear
FUNFACT:

**The native Inuit people
who live in the Arctic
call the polar bear "Nanook."**

This polar bear cub stands on its hind legs because it is curious, but it stays close to its mother to keep safe and warm.

This polar bear is cooling off on the ice. Polar bears also spread out and crawl on their stomachs to avoid breaking the ice when it is very thin.

Every year the Earth's temperature is rising a little bit. This is known as global warming. The rate of warming is at least twice as fast in the Arctic as it is in other parts of the world. This means that the ice is getting thinner and there is less of it than there was in the past.

Because the polar bear needs the ice as a place to hunt seals and other prey, global warming might cause some bears to starve to death. In Canada especially, scientists have found that more and more polar bear cubs are dying from lack of food.

This polar bear cub follows its mother in the snow. Most female
polar bears are 5 or 6 years old when they give birth to their first cubs.

Some bears in places like Churchill, Manitoba, in Canada have even roamed through town where people live. The hungry bears look for food in garbage dumps. Sometimes people have to capture them and bring them back into the wild.

Pollution (puh-LOO-shun) is another threat to polar bears. Poisonous chemicals called PCBs have found their way into the food supply of polar bears.

Another threat to polar bears is the impact that humans can have on their habitat. The Arctic National Wildlife Refuge was created in 1960 in Alaska as a protected wild area. This is one important area where mother polar bears build their dens to protect them and their newborn cubs.

This place in Alaska is rich in oil. Some people want to drill for oil in this area. But mother polar bears are very sensitive to the noise of humans. This could cause them to leave their dens or abandon their cubs. If people are allowed to drill for oil, they must be very careful to protect these bears.

Fortunately, there are people who are working to protect polar bears. Hopefully, this will help the bears to survive so there will be more of these wonderful Arctic animals in the wild.

Polar Bear
FUNFACT:

The polar bear's body temperature is 98.6 degrees Fahrenheit (37 degrees Celsius)—the same as that of humans.

Internet Sites

You can find out more interesting information about polar bears and lots of other wildlife by visiting these web sites.

http://endangered.fws.gov/kids/index.html	U.S. Fish and Wildlife Service
www.animal.discovery.com	Discovery Channel Online
www.bearbiology.com	International Association for Bear Research and Management
www.bear.org/Polar/PB_Home.html	North American Bear Center
www.EnchantedLearning.com	Enchanted Learning
www.kidsplanet.org	Defenders of Wildlife
www.learner.org/jnorth	Journey North
www.nationalgeographic.com/kids	National Geographic Society
www.nwf.org/kids	National Wildlife Federation
www.ocean.com/library/creaturefeature/	Ocean.com
www.polarbearsalive.org	Polar Bears Alive
www.tnc.org	The Nature Conservancy
www.wcs.org	Wildlife Conservation Society
www.worldwildlife.org/fun/kids.cfm	World Wildlife Fund
www.wwfcanada.org/satellite/wwfkids	Canadian World Wildlife Fund

Index

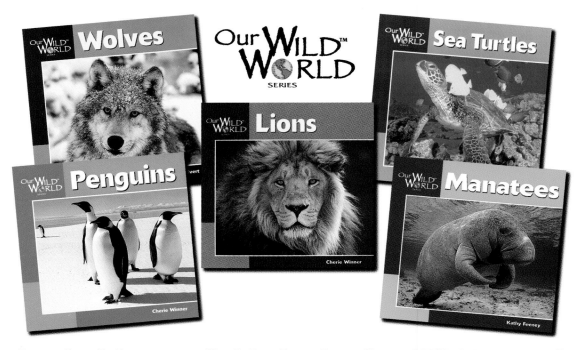

Paperback titles available in the Our Wild World Series:

BISON
ISBN 1-55971-775-0

BLACK BEARS
ISBN 1-55971-742-4

CARIBOU
ISBN 1-55971-812-9

COUGARS
ISBN 1-55971-788-2

DOLPHINS
ISBN 1-55971-776-9

EAGLES
ISBN 1-55971-777-7

LEOPARDS
ISBN 1-55971-796-3

LIONS
ISBN 1-55971-787-4

MANATEES
ISBN 1-55971-778-5

MOOSE
ISBN 1-55971-744-0

PENGUINS
ISBN 1-55971-810-2

POLAR BEARS
ISBN 1-55971-828-5

SEALS
ISBN 1-55971-826-9

SEA TURTLES
ISBN 1-55971-746-7

SHARKS
ISBN 1-55971-779-3

TIGERS
ISBN 1-55971-797-1

WHALES
ISBN 1-55971-780-7

WHITETAIL DEER
ISBN 1-55971-743-2

WOLVES
ISBN 1-55971-748-3

See your nearest bookseller, or order by phone 1-800-328-3895

NorthWord Press
Chanhassen, Minnesota